UNDERSTANDING

CANCER

BY
HOLLY DUHIG

BookLife
PUBLISHING

©2018
BookLife Publishing
King's Lynn
Norfolk PE30 4LS

Written by:
Holly Duhig

Edited by:
Kirsty Holmes

Designed by:
Drue Rintoul

CONTENTS

Words that look like **this** are explained in the glossary on page 31.

WHAT IS CANCER?

Cancer is actually a name for a group of diseases that affect the body's cells. Cells are the basic building blocks of our bodies and the bodies of all living things. There are many different types of cells in your body, each with different jobs to do. Some carry oxygen through your blood, some send messages between your body and your brain and some group together to form organs such as your heart, lungs and liver.

It is the job of all cells, however, to help keep you alive. Healthy cells do this by dividing and making copies of themselves in a controlled way that helps us to grow, heal and repair. Cancer is caused by unhealthy cells making copies of themselves in a way that is not controlled. These unhealthy cells group together to form something called a tumour.

CANCER CELLS

NORMAL CELLS

FACT

THERE ARE AROUND 210 DIFFERENT TYPES OF CELL IN THE BODY, AND THEY ALL HAVE DIFFERENT JOBS.

CANCER TUMOUR

Lots of people will either have cancer, or will know someone who does, at some point in their lifetime. Because of this, cancer gets talked about a lot on the news and doctors are always trying to find new and better ways to treat it.

Cancer is a serious disease because, if it is not treated or if it spreads very quickly, it can be **fatal**. However, nowadays people can be treated quickly and more people are recovering from cancer than ever before.

Even though it is more common in adults, children can be **diagnosed** with cancer too. However, although cancer is a serious illness, many people get better from it and go on to lead healthy lives.

TESTING FOR CANCER

If a doctor believes that someone has cancer, that person will usually need to have lots of tests done to find out for certain. This means that they will probably need to make many visits to the hospital.

This is often worrying for the family and friends of someone with cancer, but it's important to remember that these hospital visits are a good thing because they are all about trying to make people better.

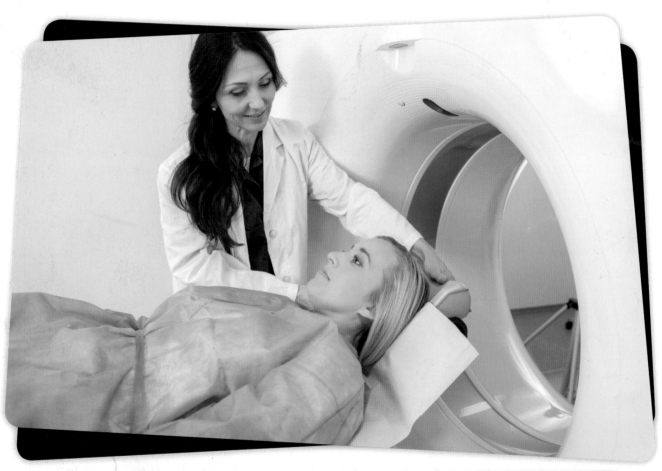

Testing for cancer might include blood tests, where a doctor will take some blood from a vein in your arm and send it away to be tested by experts. Other types of tests include x-rays and MRI scans. These scans give doctors a very detailed image of the body which will show them if there are any tumours.

X-rays and MRI scans do not hurt and are very useful for doctors. The sooner cancer is found during these tests, the easier it is to treat. If, after testing, someone is diagnosed with cancer, they will be taken care of by an oncologist (say: on-colla-jist) - a doctor that specialises in cancer treatment. Because cancer can be quite a complicated illness, an oncologist's first job will be to explain to their patient everything they need to know about their diagnosis. This includes where in their body the cancer has been found and whether or not it has spread to other parts of their body.

CELLS AND TUMOURS

Being diagnosed with cancer, or knowing someone who has, can be worrying for anybody of any age. However, understanding more about what cancer is, how it develops and how it's treated can help it to feel less frightening and more manageable.

TUMOURS

Benign Tumours

Some tumours are considered benign (say: be-nine). This means that they are not cancerous. These tumours grow slowly, don't spread and are surrounded by lots of healthy cells that help contain them.

HARMLESS BIRTHMARKS, ALSO CALLED HAEMANGIOMAS, ARE A TYPE OF BENIGN TUMOUR.

Malignant Tumours

Malignant tumours are cancerous, which means they grow out of control and are able to spread to other parts of the body. But why are these tumours so damaging to our health?

One way in which a tumour can cause damage is by destroying nearby healthy cells. If, for example, a malignant tumour began in someone's liver (the organ that cleans the blood), it might destroy the healthy cells around it and stop the liver from working. All cells, including unhealthy cells, need a supply of oxygen and **nutrients** to stay alive. To get this, cells are able to send out signals that tell the body to start making blood **vessels**. With a blood supply, a tumour can keep on growing and growing.

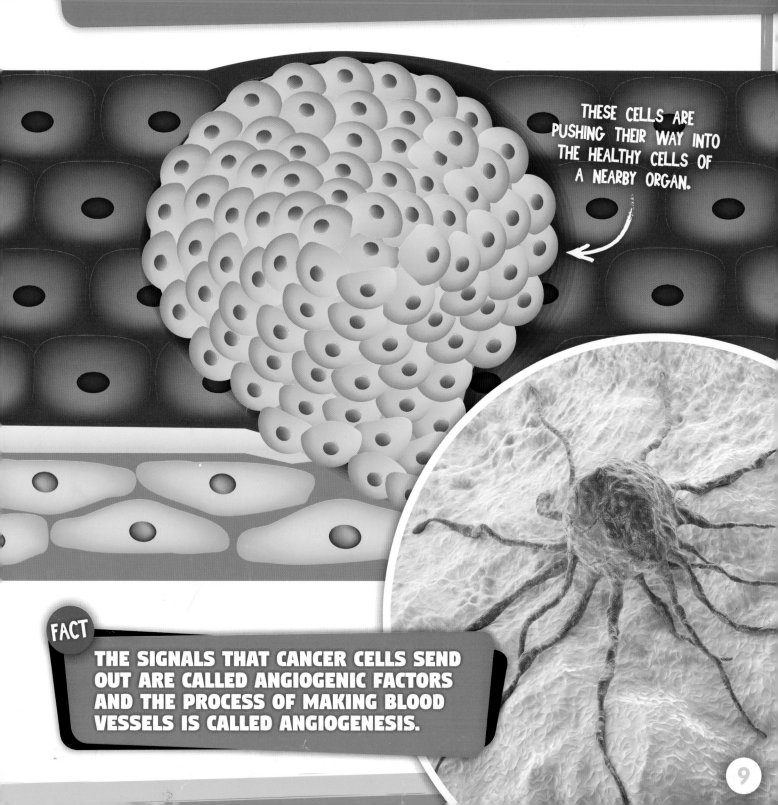

THESE CELLS ARE PUSHING THEIR WAY INTO THE HEALTHY CELLS OF A NEARBY ORGAN.

FACT

THE SIGNALS THAT CANCER CELLS SEND OUT ARE CALLED ANGIOGENIC FACTORS AND THE PROCESS OF MAKING BLOOD VESSELS IS CALLED ANGIOGENESIS.

HOW TUMOURS SPREAD

Circulatory System

Cancer tumours are able to spread around the body in many ways. One of these ways is through the system of blood vessels, veins and **arteries** called the circulatory (say: sur-cu-LATE-ur-ee) system. As cancer tumours grow bigger, they press on nearby healthy cells. As they do this, they squash the blood vessels that supply the healthy cells and cause them to starve.

This makes it even easier for the tumour to spread. Cells from the tumour may also break off from the first tumour – also known as the primary tumour – and travel through the blood vessels. Because all the blood vessels and veins in the body are connected, the cancerous cells are able to spread through the whole body.

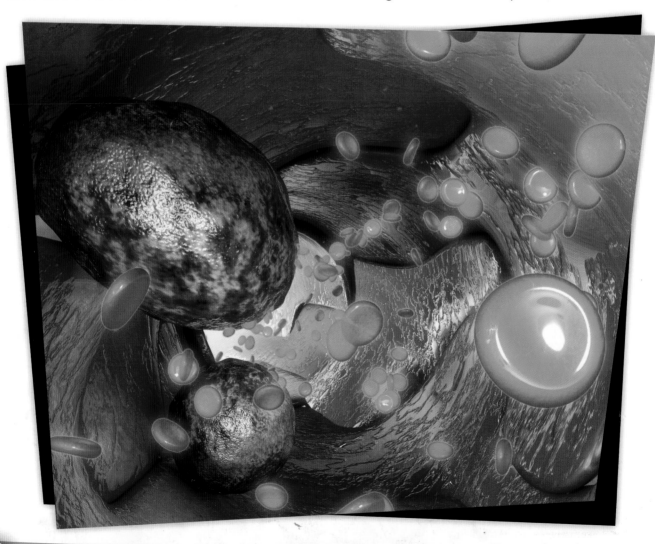

Lymphatic System

Cancer is also able to spread through the lymphatic (say: lim-fa-tic) system. This system uses vessels to take away waste, such as extra fluids and bacteria, and destroy it in places called lymph nodes. Like the circulatory system, the lymphatic system also reaches all over the body. However, it is made of much smaller vessels. Sometimes these vessels pick up and try to destroy cancer cells. Your body does this to try to protect you but it can provide another way for cancer to spread.

LYMPHATIC SYSTEM

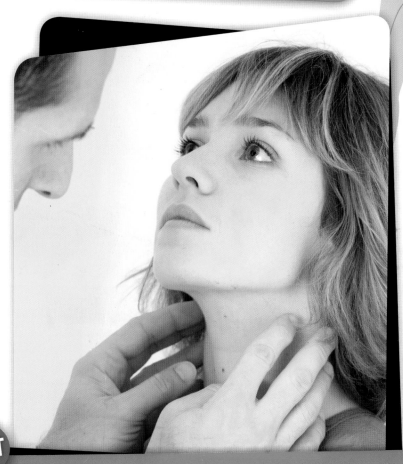

FACT

WHEN CHECKING FOR CANCER, DOCTORS OFTEN CHECK FOR SWOLLEN LYMPH NODES IN THE NECK BECAUSE THIS SHOWS THERE MIGHT BE A BUILD-UP OF CANCER CELLS.

TYPES OF CANCER

Cancer is more common in adults than in children. As people get older, their cells are not as good at dividing and growing. When children do get cancer, there are some types that are more common than others. One in every four children who have a tumour have it on their brain or **spinal cord**. These tumours are usually non-cancerous. However, we don't call them benign because, even though they aren't cancer, they can cause damage to very important parts of the body.

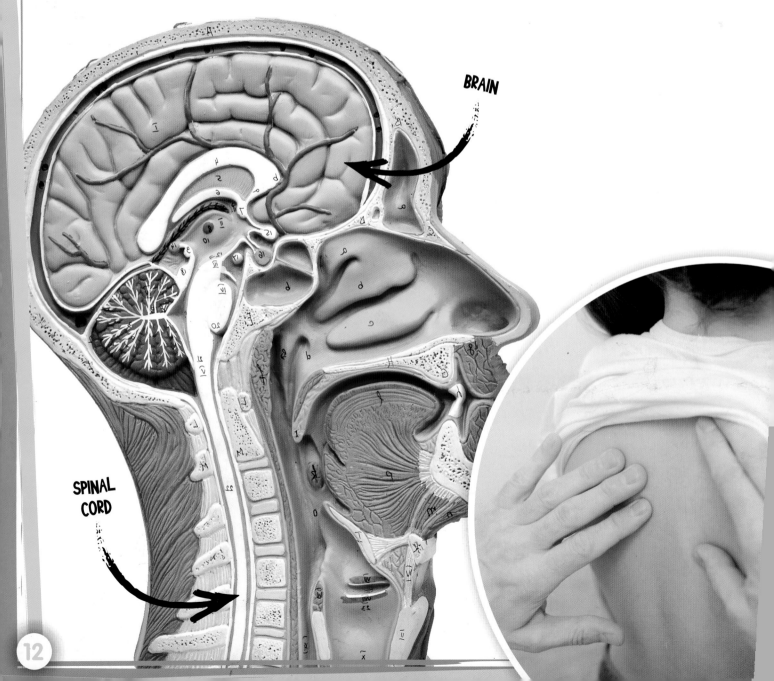

BRAIN

SPINAL CORD

Brain Tumours

A brain tumour can have lots of different symptoms depending on where in the brain it grows. If it grows in the cerebrum – the part of your brain that controls emotions, language and some movements – it can cause symptoms such as **seizures**, speech problems, and **paralysis**. The spinal cord is responsible for sending signals from your brain to your body and back again. How much of the body is affected by a spinal cord tumour depends on how far up the spine the tumour is found.

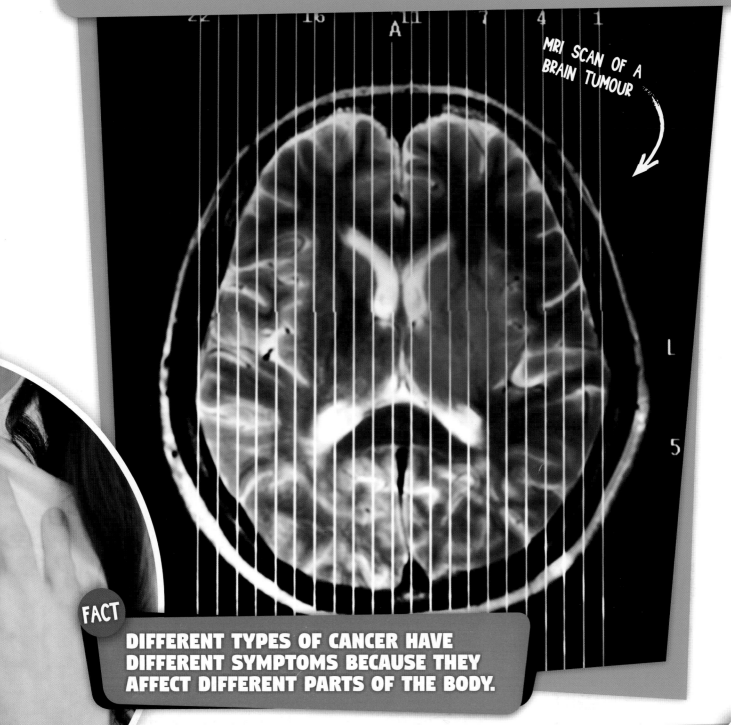

MRI SCAN OF A BRAIN TUMOUR

FACT

DIFFERENT TYPES OF CANCER HAVE DIFFERENT SYMPTOMS BECAUSE THEY AFFECT DIFFERENT PARTS OF THE BODY.

LEUKAEMIA

Leukaemia (say: loo-KEE-mee-ya) is a cancer that affects the blood-making cells in our bodies. Blood is made in the soft, inner part of our bones, called our bone marrow. In the bone marrow, there are lots of cells called stem cells, waiting to be turned into blood cells. There are two types of blood cells: red blood cells and white blood cells. Cell **fragments**, called platelets, are also made in the bone marrow.

White blood cells travel round our bodies and help fight off germs and infections. Leukaemia is a cancer of these white blood cells. It means that your body is making lots of **faulty** white blood cells that can't do their job properly. When these cells grow out of control, they stop your body from being able to make red blood cells. Red blood cells are important because they carry oxygen around your body.

LEUKAEMIA WHITE BLOOD CELLS

FACT

ONE IN EVERY THREE CHILDREN WHO ARE DIAGNOSED WITH CANCER HAVE LEUKAEMIA.

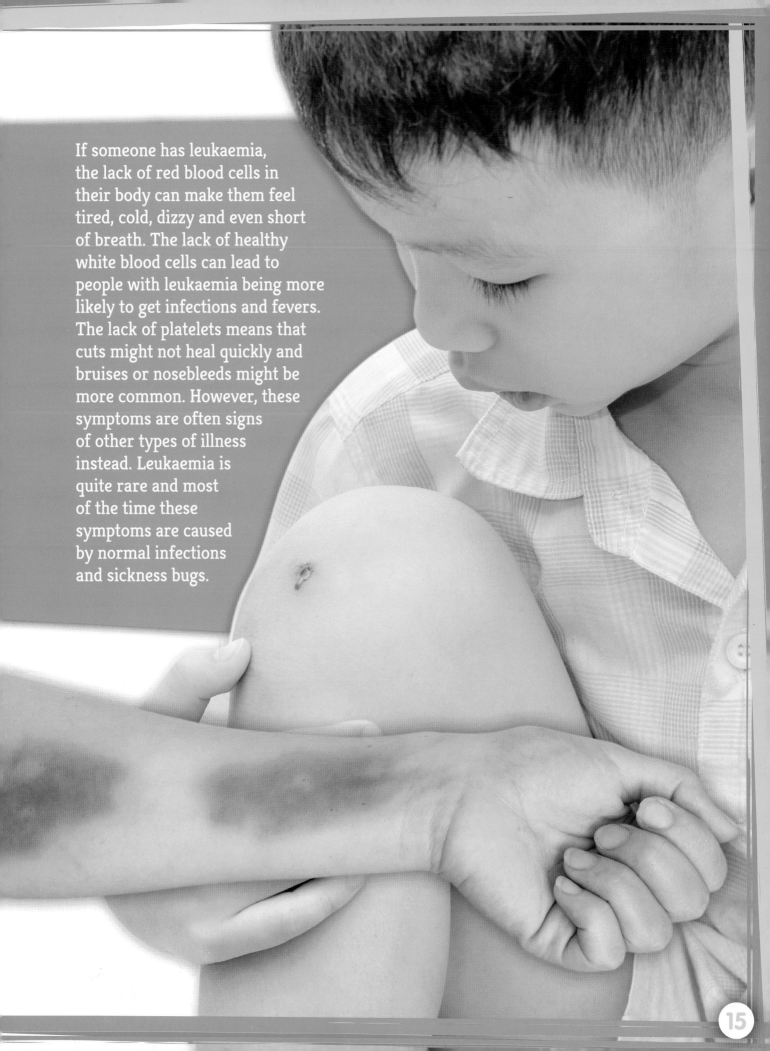

If someone has leukaemia, the lack of red blood cells in their body can make them feel tired, cold, dizzy and even short of breath. The lack of healthy white blood cells can lead to people with leukaemia being more likely to get infections and fevers. The lack of platelets means that cuts might not heal quickly and bruises or nosebleeds might be more common. However, these symptoms are often signs of other types of illness instead. Leukaemia is quite rare and most of the time these symptoms are caused by normal infections and sickness bugs.

TREATMENTS

There are lots of treatments for all types of cancer and these are constantly being improved upon by doctors and scientists. One of the main treatments for cancer, which most people have heard of, is called chemotherapy (say: kee-mo-THER-a-pee), often called chemo (say: kee-mo) for short. Chemotherapy is a type of cancer treatment that uses drugs and medicine that are cytotoxic, which means cell-killing.

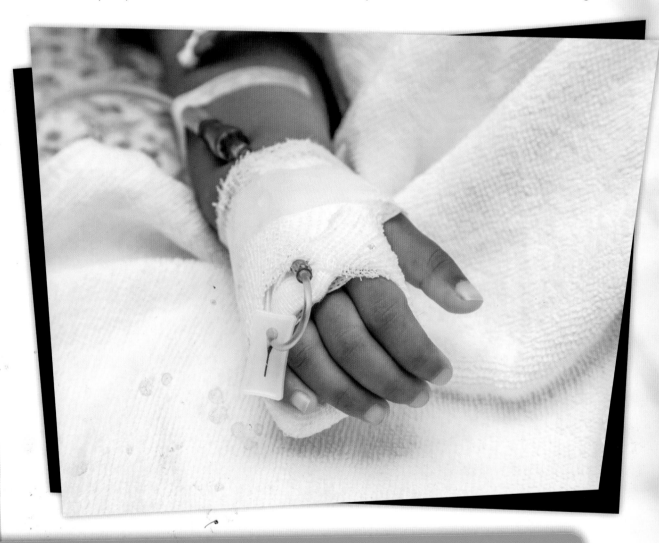

There are many different types of chemotherapy drugs and many ways they can be delivered to your body. Some chemotherapy drugs are given straight into your veins. This can be done at the hospital using a cannula. This is a tube which goes into a vein in the back of your hand or arm, and is taken out by a doctor before you go home.

IT IS COMMON TO FEEL TIRED AFTER TAKING CHEMOTHERAPY DRUGS.

There are also ways of delivering chemotherapy drugs to patients at home. This allows people who have cancer to get on with their normal day-to-day lives while being treated. One of the most common ways of treating cancer at home is through a pump that is connected to a patient's arm or chest. This pump can be carried in a bag or on a belt.

A doctor or nurse will teach the patient, as well as their family or caregivers, how to take care of their pump at home. Other chemotherapy treatments include having injections into the fluid around your spine and taking drugs orally (by swallowing them). This is often done to treat brain tumours and leukaemia.

SIDE EFFECTS

Chemotherapy kills cancer cells, but it also kills healthy cells too. This can lead to lots of **temporary** side effects. One of the most noticeable side effects of chemotherapy is hair loss. Hair loss is often thought to be a symptom of cancer, but it is actually a side effect of cancer treatment. Hair loss happens because chemotherapy kills the cells under the skin that make hair grow. For both children and adults with cancer, losing their hair can often be quite upsetting. However, it's important to remember that hair loss is only happening because of drugs that are helping people get better.

FACT

SOME PEOPLE WITH CANCER GET SHORT HAIRCUTS OR USE HEADSCARVES, HATS AND WIGS TO HIDE THEIR HAIR LOSS, WHILE OTHERS DON'T. IT IS ALL DOWN TO PERSONAL CHOICE.

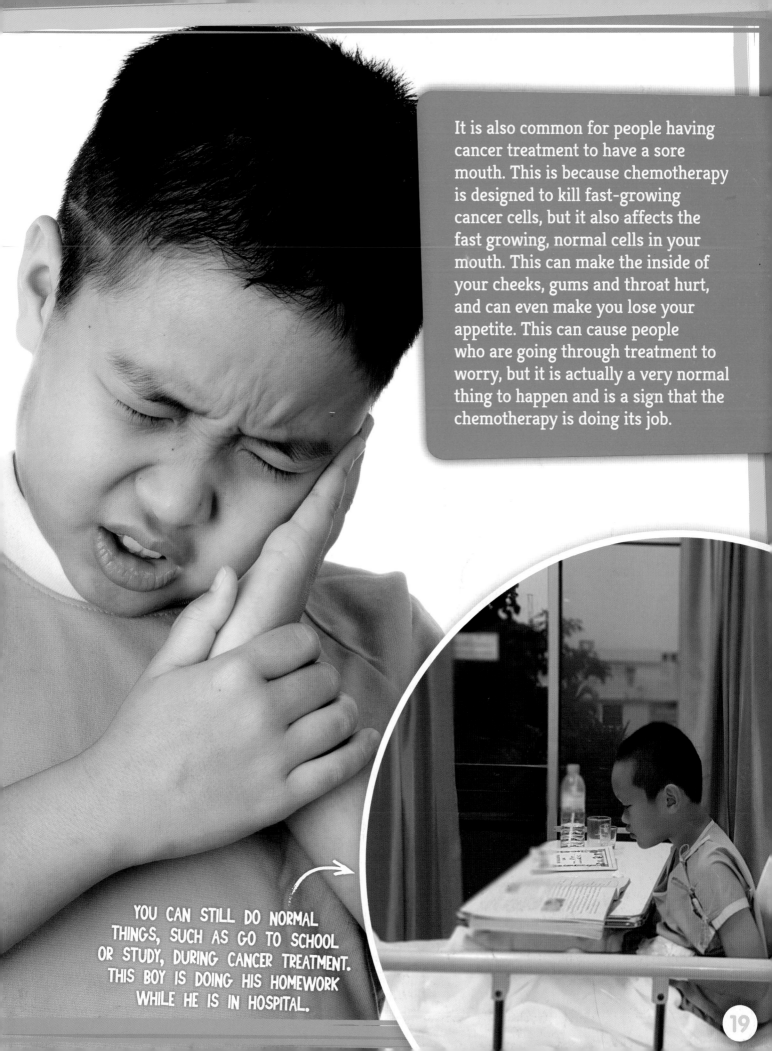

It is also common for people having cancer treatment to have a sore mouth. This is because chemotherapy is designed to kill fast-growing cancer cells, but it also affects the fast growing, normal cells in your mouth. This can make the inside of your cheeks, gums and throat hurt, and can even make you lose your appetite. This can cause people who are going through treatment to worry, but it is actually a very normal thing to happen and is a sign that the chemotherapy is doing its job.

YOU CAN STILL DO NORMAL THINGS, SUCH AS GO TO SCHOOL OR STUDY, DURING CANCER TREATMENT. THIS BOY IS DOING HIS HOMEWORK WHILE HE IS IN HOSPITAL.

CASE STUDY: MIRANDA

My name is Miranda. I am nine years old and I have leukaemia. I had been feeling poorly and tired for a while before I was diagnosed by my doctor. Mum and Dad took me to the doctor when my tummy started looking **bloated**. The doctor explained that I was feeling tired because my body was trying to fight cancer and that it was the cancer that was making my tummy swell up. I didn't really know what cancer was at first but I knew it was serious. My doctor explained it to me very well and that made me feel much better.

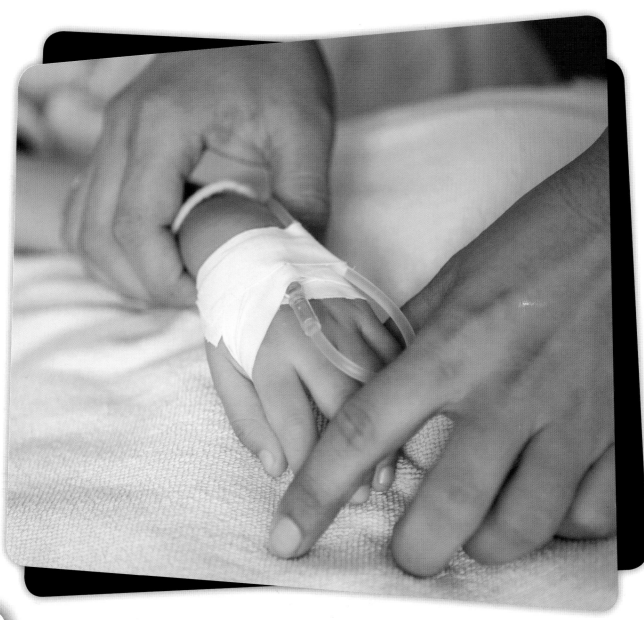

My treatment included chemotherapy as well as lots of blood transfusions, which is where a doctor puts blood from a **donor** into my body so that I don't run out of red blood cells. My treatment seemed to go on for ages and it was very difficult at times. I kept thinking that it wasn't fair. Why did I have to get cancer? My friends took very good care of me but having cancer made me feel different. Because of this, I saw a **counsellor** who helped me talk about how I was feeling.

I was going through treatment for a long time but eventually my cancer started getting better. I still have to go to the hospital for check-ups and treatments to make sure the cancer doesn't come back but things seem to be looking up.

I WORE A HAT DURING MY TREATMENT TO COVER MY HAIR WHEN IT STARTED FALLING OUT.

TALKING ABOUT YOUR FEELINGS

Having someone close to you be diagnosed with cancer, or being diagnosed yourself, can be an emotional experience. Some people with cancer feel scared or even angry. Nobody deserves to be ill, and it can feel very unfair when you or someone you love gets sick. Talking to someone you trust, like a parent or carer, can help you to feel better. Some people also choose to talk to a counsellor. Some counsellors are experts in helping people who are going through illnesses like cancer.

FACT

KEEPING A DIARY OR WRITING LETTERS TO YOUR LOVED ONES CAN HELP GET THE FEELINGS THAT ARE IN YOUR HEAD OUT ON PAPER.

If you have cancer, it can help to talk to other people who are going through it too. Some hospitals will have **support groups** where you can talk to people the same age as you who are going through similar treatments.

When someone close to you has cancer, you might feel like you don't want to add to their worries by talking to them about yours. This might stop you from talking openly about how you feel. However, talking openly is helpful for everybody; it can let your loved ones know that you care and that you are there for them. Talking can also help the friends and families of people with cancer to share their worries.

MORE TREATMENTS

Radiation Therapy

Radiation therapy is a type of cancer treatment that uses high-energy x-rays or **gamma rays** to shrink tumours and kill cancer cells. Unlike chemotherapy, which affects the whole body, radiation therapy affects the tumour directly. This means it can focus on the tumour cells and not damage as many healthy cells. It can also help shrink cancer tumours that are causing blockages in the body. For example, a tumour in the lungs can make breathing and exercising very difficult, so radiation therapy could help to shrink or kill the tumour so the patient feels better.

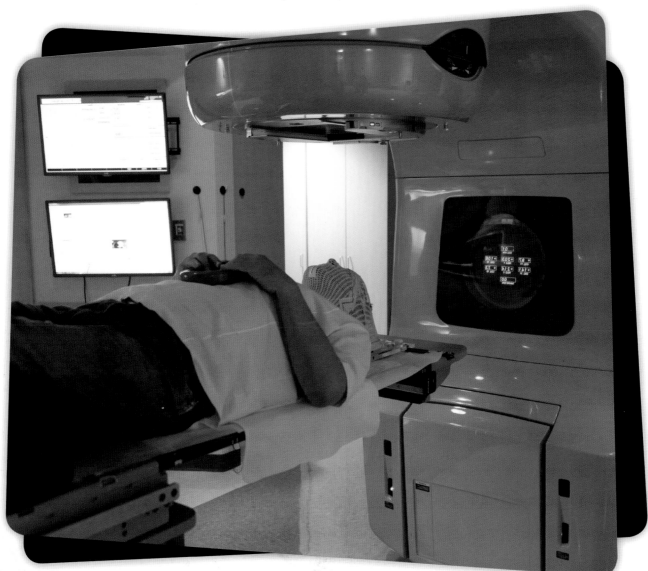

Stem Cell Transplants

Stem cells, like the ones in bone marrow, are a type of cell that don't have a specific job. They are very useful in treating cancer because they can be made into any type of cell the body needs. Stem cells can be given to a cancer patient by a donor and they can help your body to recover after treatments like chemotherapy and radiotherapy. Stem cell transplants are especially useful for treating leukaemia because, when injected into the blood of a cancer patient, the donor's healthy stem cells can attack the patient's cancer cells.

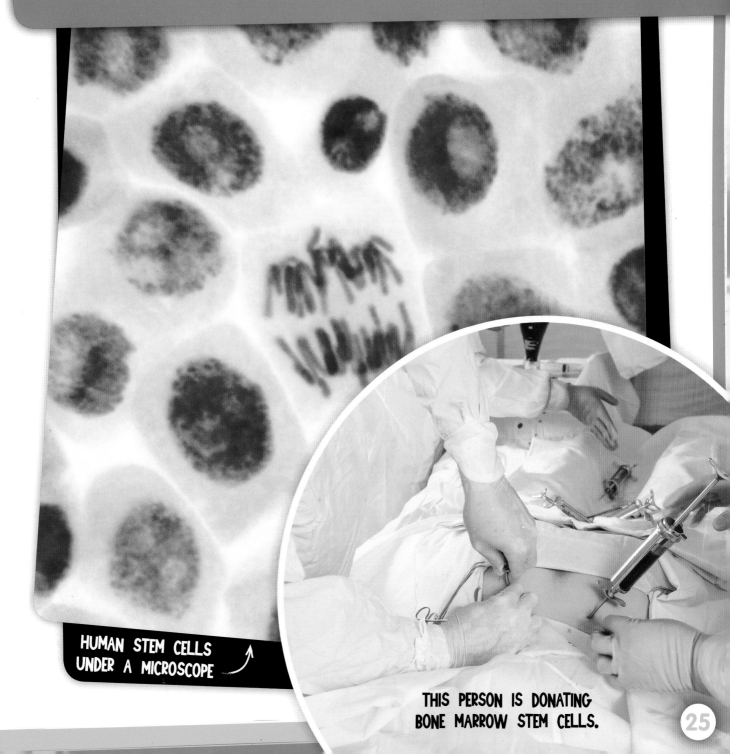

HUMAN STEM CELLS UNDER A MICROSCOPE

THIS PERSON IS DONATING BONE MARROW STEM CELLS.

CASE STUDY: CHRISTINA

My name is Christina and my mum's name is Julie. My mum used to have cancer. The doctors say she is in **remission** now which means the doctors can't find any more cancer in her body. When my mum was sick, I felt really scared. I couldn't concentrate on my school work because I was so worried about my mum. I used to get scared whenever anyone talked about cancer at home and I would run upstairs to my room. I just wanted everything to go back to normal.

One day mum took me to the hospital with her so that I could meet the doctors who were taking care of her. They told me about everything they were doing to try to help my mum's cancer go away. The doctor told me that my mum was a very strong lady and that her body was fighting cancer really well. They told me that my mum had breast cancer but that it hadn't spread anywhere else and that this was a good sign. I felt much less scared after talking to the doctor. Mum had chemotherapy as well as an operation and now she is much better. Her hair has even started growing back! This year we are both doing a **sponsored** run to help raise money for cancer charities.

CANCER RESEARCH

Cancer affects many people and their families. Because of this, lots of research has been done into finding newer and better treatments for it. Scientists are hopeful that new research and technology will lead to more effective cancer treatments and maybe one day even a cure.

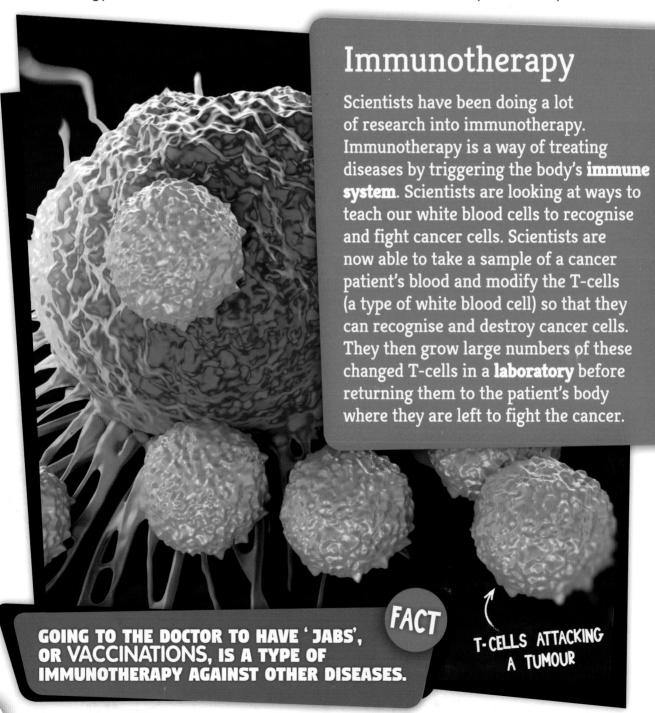

Immunotherapy

Scientists have been doing a lot of research into immunotherapy. Immunotherapy is a way of treating diseases by triggering the body's **immune system**. Scientists are looking at ways to teach our white blood cells to recognise and fight cancer cells. Scientists are now able to take a sample of a cancer patient's blood and modify the T-cells (a type of white blood cell) so that they can recognise and destroy cancer cells. They then grow large numbers of these changed T-cells in a **laboratory** before returning them to the patient's body where they are left to fight the cancer.

FACT

GOING TO THE DOCTOR TO HAVE 'JABS', OR VACCINATIONS, IS A TYPE OF IMMUNOTHERAPY AGAINST OTHER DISEASES.

T-CELLS ATTACKING A TUMOUR

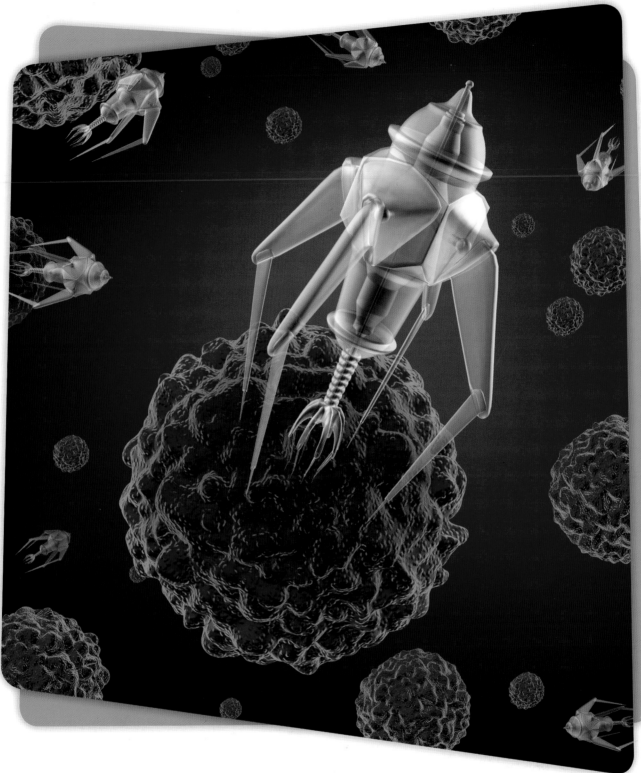

Nanotechnology

Nanotechnology is technology smaller than 100 **nanometres**. Scientists are working on developing nanoparticles that can attach to cancer tumours and deliver chemotherapy drugs to them without harming the rest of the body. Scientists also hope that, instead of delivering drugs, nanoparticles can be sent to tumours and then heated by lasers until they explode. This explosion will be so small that it will only kill the cancer cells, and not the healthy cells around it.

DONATIONS AND FUNDRAISING

Of course, cancer research like this takes lots of time and needs lots of money. None of these life-saving discoveries would be possible without donations and fundraising from people who want to find a cure for cancer faster. There are lots of charities all around the world that are set up to care for people affected by cancer or to help fund research projects to find cures for cancer.

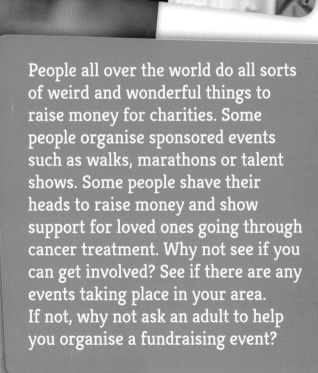

People all over the world do all sorts of weird and wonderful things to raise money for charities. Some people organise sponsored events such as walks, marathons or talent shows. Some people shave their heads to raise money and show support for loved ones going through cancer treatment. Why not see if you can get involved? See if there are any events taking place in your area. If not, why not ask an adult to help you organise a fundraising event?

GLOSSARY

arteries	tubes that carry blood away from the heart and to the rest of the body
bloated	swollen with fluid or gas
counsellor	a person who is specially trained to listen and give advice
diagnosed	when a disease or illness is identified by a doctor
donor	a person who donates their healthy blood, organs or stem cells to help others
fatal	able to cause death
faulty	not working or made correctly
fragments	tiny, broken pieces
gamma rays	a type of electromagnetic radiation
immune system	the body's defence against illness
laboratory	a room or building used by scientists to conduct experiments and research
nanometres	units of measurement equal to one billionth of a metre
nutrients	natural substances that people need to grow and stay healthy
paralysis	being unable to move part or all of your body
remission	a decrease in or disappearance of signs and symptoms of cancer
seizures	sudden uncontrolled electrical activity in the brain
spinal cord	the cord of nervous tissue that extends from the brain and through the backbone
sponsored	to support a person, organization, or activity by giving money
support groups	groups of people with similar experiences who come together for support and comfort
temporary	only lasting for a short time
vaccinations	treatments designed to make someone immune to a certain disease
vessels	tubes in the body

INDEX